The Father of the Predicaments

WESLEYAN POETRY

Heather McHugh

THE FATHER
OF THE
PREDICAMENTS

Wesleyan University Press

Published by University Press of New England

Hanover and London

Wesleyan University Press

Published by University Press of New England, Hanover, NH 03755

© 1999 by Heather McHugh

5   4   3   2   1

CIP data appear at the end of the book

Contents

Not a Prayer

. . . she is nourished for a time, and times, and half a time, from the face of a serpent.
—Revelations 12:14

✧

We sleep inside a bullet —
cheek to cheek, in public
anonymity — and then we wake. We do

not speak. The sun's
a red-eye, and the earth
a fast blue rushing underneath.

✧

"You've come into my life," she says. And then
"I want for you to understand." A night
and a day and a night from then,

I'd understand all right, helping to hook
around her corpse's chin and ears
the strap that keeps

a speaking-place from gaping.

✧

Throughout the daylong night, the nightlong day, the livelong time
that's left, we mean to be her mates, go anywhere she drifts — we'd fol-
low every surge of language, every scrap and flotsam — give up every
tillerwork for her, if she required. But what does she require? The
place has no coordinates — or else it's we who don't — who fall asleep
to jerk awake at her every "Are you there?" or "What are we?" or, now
and then, her half-polite, half-consternatious Russian-French
"*Pardon?*"

✧

"Malheureusement, pour être mort,
il faut mourir." And now we tangle up
the nightgown's arm; can't get the air-tubes
through the head-hole; all of us are clumsy,
short on sleep and snapping at each other —
she emitting cries of naked fear and
sheer indignity. Oh for the calm
credentials of a nurse, the competences
of a nurse, the cool! But when
the nurse, a family friend, arrives

a clamor comes from in the room —
the nurse has been mistaken for
someone her husband cheated with
a thousand years ago, and now
his wife "won't have her in the house."
It seems we have to die the way we lived.
The nurse departs, and love,
that history of strangleholds,
has left her with
the likes of us.

✧

At first the impulse was to finish up her falterings. "You know . . . you
know . . ." she tried a hundred times. "Know what?" her son kept prob-
ing, but she couldn't say. One knew it took some life from her to try.

✧

Who tells the time?
A calibration's on the shelf,
syringe her husband wouldn't give her.
She is not in pain, he says, and he's
the doctor. Two days from today
(is it today?) I took the red-eye. One

AM: is anyone awake? Arrived
a life ago. But time is going
to be unkept. It has
to tell itself.

✧

The body is moved from its chair onto the cart.
The head is calm. It has, for once in seven decades,
no more mask of lipstick and mascara. Now I see:
she's beautiful. Each eyebrow exquisite,
and every lash. Her mother must have felt
precisely this objective an affection, when her own
long day and night of laboring were over. Then

the black bag's zipper rips
the seeing from my sight.

✧

To put some sense together, she takes
time: ten minutes, twenty, half an hour.
The others come and go.
Each thinks her thinking
incoherent. But if anybody
listens long enough he hears
(among the many dozings)
something terribly intelligible.

"Yesterday yesterday I was [and here she falls asleep for seven minutes]
yesterday I was full of new [she falls asleep for three] new life new life
but today but today new life but today [she falls asleep eleven minutes]
I am full of full of yesterday I was [she falls asleep] was full of new life
but today I am full of of [come back, come back, I tell one of her sons,
the sentence has a structure, when she falls asleep she's not forgetting]
but today [she falls asleep, he can't believe me] I am full of but today
I'm full of [somebody is calling him from somewhere else and then

he's gone] but today I am full of . . . [now she'll tell me, now I'll know]
. . . I'm full of finished ..."

[Full of finished? is that last word AFTER the ellipsis? should it be
attached to how, instead of what, she meant? which parts were talking
about talking, should I put some
quotes in quotes? some kind
of mind inside the mind, some
time inside, or out? or what? This bracket

is the writer's. Who
are you? are you? are you?]

✧

Her husband is her caretaker, and he's half-deaf. The conferences he
ought to whisper with his sons, about some undertakerly details, turn
out to be a yelling kind of telling — she can hear: her eyes snap open.
Leaning fast into her frequencies, I chant

some species of a muffling song: "Don't worry, everything will be OK,
everything will be OK," the hymn I used to use when my own mother
wept, my father threw his plate against the wall. The father of the
predicaments, wrote Aristotle's translator, is being. Yes, but nothing
you can translate can be true. So when the powers of the universe have
got

the future all wrapped up again, I lean back from her ear and repossess
my listening-spot, here at the foot of her chair, at the tip of her hand.
She wets her lips. She's saying something.

"Everything," she says.

✧

The days of oi-oi-oi have passed
into the days of oh — (when even a diphthong
taxed too much) — and then the oh-oh-oh
to hours of ah, the ah
to hours of of. And then
for some one hundred minutes more she made
an of that sounded something

like an awe — but with
a hitch. Awe plus a gasp,
a flutter, fell. For hours it was
awful awful awful. (Who knows if, and at what price,

she tried to tell us something with that extra syllable?
Or was it just the lung mechanic's mockery? How tell
a word from senselessness, a grown-up from his
homonym?) One son (aged 49) kept calling "Mama"

and by reflex first and then enormous effort,
she would wrench herself from somewhere far away
to heed his cry. It seemed too much to ask:
the cry itself was all he had to say. We listened way
too hard, and one took notes.

✧

For the rest of his life, he'll relive the scene. She furious: "You did not
get me morphine?" He: "I can't, I can't." He says it every day, until she
cannot spare the air to speak.

At last his sons prevail on him to find her one syringe at least, and so he
has to make the calls, do paperwork in triplicate, get signatures from
several fellow-doctors, and secure the morphine from the pharmacy —
when most he doesn't want to leave her side.

And still the morphine is not used. The night wears on. "She feels no
pain" becomes his theme, his hope, his surety, his dream.

Eventually this painlessness becomes unbearable, and even he agrees
a merciful, not mortal, dosage should be given. Hands trembling, head
a blur from four days' watchfulness and grief, and eighty years of hu-
man work and love, he comes to this: the moment to swab her arm,
and shoot the shot. Each son takes in a slow deep breath — and then
can't let it out. The drug has swelled into a gruesome pocket under-
neath her skin — it never hits the vein. This blue-black bulge is an af-
front her husband covers quickly with his hand. And holds that arm
down for the rest of her life. The whole night long. While her free arm
flails.

✧

What's worse?
To know? Or not to know?
I've been a little cuckoo, she
woke up and, waking,
said. But when she wasn't
saying anything, what ravens
settled in her head?

✧

I thought I would be earth-struck, terrified,
there in the body's room with nobody,
or only a body, by my side. Instead

her calm's my haven — most especially
from the swarm of friends who loved
her bright society, and so

assemble in the aftermath. Each visitor
dips once into the study's
pool of quiet, where she lies

so self-absorbed, preoccupied —
then flees toward the living,
in the living room.

I'm free to stroke her face, to register
its "cold" or "marble" meaning.
Contrary to all the stories, it is not

a statue's surface, although indisputable beneath her skin
is some enormous cool, immovable. She's not
a headstone but a model. Not an idea: an ideal. It's reverence,

it's not revulsion, that I feel — fraternity not fright —
that is, until a photograph of her distracts me,
and I turn my back. (You shouldn't let a body out of sight.)

✧

If ever I fell asleep, the plane
would plummet from the sky. And so
I kept the watch. That's how
I kept them all alive.

✧

"But couldn't you do something with that hair?" she'd ask
my whirlwinds of arrival into town, and then she'd tell
the story of the artist in the House of Commons,
at whose entrance "every member rose."
(For all her salt, she was the true
aristocrat.) Her husband (socialist
and cardiologist, a man whose mechanisms
of association turn the humorous
to something like a legbone) resorts instead
to lecturing: "We ought to leave our bodily
remains to research." (He's not only deaf,
he's serious: the hospitals need corpses.) This was all

a thousand years ago, before I knew
the first thing about time. "Not me," was her
old come-back. "Don't think I've forgotten
all your tales of what those students do

at autopsies, touch football all about
the bed, with human body parts —
just lop it off and lob it here and there
about the abattoir. No thank you,
kolitchka. Not THIS grey head."

✧

She came out of the first night's coma, spoke, took pleasure in her
food, was terrifyingly rapacious, glazed of eye, amazing to behold:
could walk toward and from the table, raise her own reclining chair;
she glowed, she wolfed her bread and brie. A meal was called for, she'd
regained her famous appetite. To do the culinary honors, someone
delegated me.

You'd have to know the decades she had dazzled at that house. You'd
have to know the spirit of the mealtimes, and the easy gift for guests,
the zest of wit, the tellingness of taste . . .

I racked my brains: no way. I fished for thoughts. I got a ray. I thought
of fish. OK. So far so good. And then I ought, I reasoned, spare the
spice. (She wasn't speaking, hadn't spoken. Had no voice in things.) So
who was I, to make such intimate decisions ? Upstart in her kitchen,
and outsider in her kin, how could anybody come across but as intru-
sion? (Wasn't everything too crude, too delicate?) I made the fish. She
tried a fork. And then she tried another. (Now the happy family
smiled.) A third, and I could breathe again. And then the snake of
speech was stirred.

It said: "But where's the sauce?"

✧

The notes remained where she had left them,
in the living room, upon the music stand. "Shaping a sound.
Feeling a pulse. Rising and falling me-
lodic rhythm." All her breathing
having stopped, her hand

10

was bound to move.

✧

We talked our time away around her figure in the silent chair, we
missed our Madame Raconteuse. Compulsively she lifted now one,
now another, finger to her lips, and then I saw her lips were dessicated,
chapstick wasn't doing much — "Perhaps you want your lipstick?" Yes,
she nodded, yes yes yes. The onlookers applauded.

So I brought that red-gold item from the room that was her room, and
knelt beside her and began to put it on, propping my fist against her
cheek, the artist with an audience, afraid to do it badly (and so failing
as an artist) — hardly 10 days in my life had I put make-up on myself!
— and so she took the lipstick from my hand and started her own old
and daily exercise — and then "you didn't bring my mirror" she ac-
cused and everyone applauded once again.

I ran for the hand-mirror, into it she fell intent and finished off the bot-
tom lip and then she let the mirror fall, I knelt and looked into her
countenance, full-front, and saw

a suffering face, with one red lip...

"Now press your lips together" — here I tried to ape the lipstick-kiss
the lipstick-ladies do — and then her eyes raised slowly toward me,
past me, to a focus in the nowhere. Into air's enormous glass, she sent
the reddened question: "Who are you? Who *are* you? Who are you?"

✧

The room her room (no room to breathe), its lights her light,
its voice her voice, its company her company,
of her, of her, of her,
became bereft.

The glass stopped looking for her.

Two men came, in kinds of uniform, the one of law,
the other chimney-sweep or butler — ceremonial silk scarf
a blinding billowing in white. So long she'd labored
there with us, so long she'd kept
ahead of them, but now
they'd overtaken her,

they took her yellow self out of its chair
(the botched arm underneath a blanket).
I give HIM, remarked the scarf,
inclining toward the badge,
the heavy end. I always do. (He meant the head.)
I felt somewhere — indignant, delicate —
Pardon? was being said.

✧

"I tell the world that you're my daughter,"
she kept telling me, until it seemed
I had to be the world to her. Of course that wasn't true.
She had her sons and husband, grandchildren, a lifetime's friends,
adoring and adored. She had
her druthers, too, for fully half
of mankind had deserved

her darker epithets: sveenya or potz,
durak, muzheek. Somewhere between, the hapless shmuggadorehs.
The better half were her admirers, and our names

were swolinka, and svolitschka,
were putschkala and kotchkala,
were kola, bubeleh, and Heatherchik.

✧

It hurt my heart it horrified my head, that blunt
"Who are you?" spoken to my face.
And so: "I'm not myself today," I said.

✧

Somewhere deep in one unending time (through which
no thought seemed utterable) up she sat
and said in perfect clarity "I have to speak to Martha."

One son ran to tell her husband — she has spoken! — but the husband
answered "It's delirium, she hasn't anything to say to Martha,
they've not talked in years. Ignore it, it will pass." And that

was when I did, if I say so myself,
my one courageous act — who had
so failed her in the larger courages, had found
no morphine we could ease her with, no opiating words,
nothing to soothe but only temporize — who when she asked us
"Am I dying?" offered after an excruciating silence
only "We don't know. Can you tell us?" —

(my God, if that's
not cruelty, it's cowardice!) — but she
(who comprehended my incomprehension)
answered then for all of us "No one
knows death." I did, I say,
my one good thing

that moment when I turned
to the son of the man who believed
she had nothing to say, and said: "My dear,
if you don't dial up Martha, tell her that her friend is dying,
and has asked for her, and may not have the strength to talk, I swear

I'll kill you." And thereupon the son
despite his father's bidding did

find Martha's number, lift the phone
and whisper to his mom: "It's Martha,
mother, here is Martha on the phone."
Long seconds passed: I leaned
toward her ear and heard

the voice of Martha in the cellphone saying tinily:
"We love you, dearest friend; we love your love of life,"
and leaning back I saw upon that listening face
some wild emotions, efforts, tearings of intent,
attempts to speak — and then

there burst out from her voicebox
words — or rather, one word cried
three times — so loud
the others all came running from
their rooms): GOODBYE
GOODBYE GOODBYE

✧

A scrawl upon the music stand,
a passage in her hand, her hand, her hand
(excerpted from another's): "The musician

who struggles with words
in order to translate
musical meaning
into non-musical language

does so at his or her own peril."

✧

"Take care of him, take care of him," she told the cold black phone.

✧

There came a time she needed all her body to inhale — both shoulders rose convulsively to take those breaths — so frail and humping up and down like that — and suddenly I understood the first sad human being who imagined wings emergent, urgently, from flesh . . .

But meanwhile he, her man, whose faith lay in a likelihood and not a likeness, he who had said "She has nothing to say," stood by her side at last, narrating, in his best clinician's tones, what happened there before our eyes, how all those heavings of the shoulders were a patient's last few breaths, but meanwhile standing there above her chair he seemed to be holding, with his own left hand, her jawbone up — the last few breaths were being pressed between her teeth and then the mouth was shut (one son was hissing urgently "What is he doing? Why would he be doing that?"), but you could guess

she'd hate to freeze there with an open mouthhole, and I knew the father knew it, he who now was telling her extraordinary story's end, the stoic scientist she leaned upon, her rock of reason now reciting "That's the swallow, it's involuntary, that's the gulping sound they make when they are actually dead" but tears (I've never seen him cry) are streaming down his face and dropping in her hair. And then he says "My life is finished."

✧

"Kate tear off him, Hate care of vim, . . ." — she's getting tangled
in the language, there's the very
devil in it, so I have

to pry the black receiver from her hand —
"Don't worry, honey, she'll have heard
the first time right: we'll all

take care."

✧

The dining room's become
a mill of business, wheel of paperwork and news.
In short, it has become the outside world. They're calling
Shulamith, they're calling Slava (where's that number in
St. Petersburg?). They're ringing up the New York Times, which had
her notice ready years ago. (Who was it, once, defined the obit desk —
emotion anticipated in tranquility?) And in the middle of

the bustling of the redoubtable now

there's someone quiet
knocking, at the door: it is
her handyman. He's come, he says,
"to pay my last respects.
She was the only one
who ever called me a genius."

✧

Remember me. Remember me. Remember me, but oh
forget my fate.

✧

My turn on watch: the household sleeps.
But she is endlessly awake, or endlessly beyond
alternatives. Now she is lifting one hand
up toward her mouth to take
a great big bite from — ah! — an apple:
very gesture of good health. Except

there is no apple. Dying, she's become a mime.
She bites down hard on it: but it is nothing: her expression
metamorphoses from casual to mystified. With furrowed brow
and twice-examinined hand, she tries again — and then again,
again, again — with all
her concentration focussed

there, to no avail. What does
one do? Remind her what she has in hand

is thinner than the air? (How cruel must a human being be?)
But now, thank God, begins a new employment—
then it too becomes, by God, another kind
of curse, a more and more
obsessive scraping at
her own left thumbnail, stubbornly,
as if to peel the whole thing off. And now she's getting
frustrated. And now (dear God, expensive God!) she's asking for a knife . . .

✧

After the all-night labor, through the course of which
nobody could protect or soothe her, none contain
the messages in words (each effort getting
shredded, every speech-quilt
left in tatters, all our best
and all our least
capacities out-ripped) there yet
will come another pure and
vintage sentence from her lips. At 5 AM
the day we call the day-before-the-last:

"I'm finding it hard

to express myself —", then one beat later

"— after all, I'm no philosopher."

✧

Wheelchair parked by the piano,
one hand on my arm, confidingly (for we
are quite alone): "You know, you know, you know . . ." and then —
(without a single balk or reservation) she begins to hum a tune —

some six or seven measures of
a piece I do indeed know well,
I even hum a while along.
But what I know

I know by love,
and not by heart's
remoter rote: I know
its course, and not its name —

and without that, and without her,
or anybody else to be my witness,
because God apparently is not — and if he were,
he would not help us, because God (as Cioran says) can't read —

and lacking first the name and now
the sound as well— because for me
a sound's a time and time's an unrecoverable flow—
because of all of that, and more, I can't
begin to tell you (cannot call
to mind again, I fear, for
study, or for love, or for the life of me)
what people always want to know —

what did she mean? All I can call upon
is words — unsatisfactory to say
the least — a nomen always aiming
for amen, a pupil meaning
well, pre-emptively.
For what she sang
that time of times

no soul remembers to foresee.

Not Unterrified

Edge-rich, the beach
is a batcher of changes:
five long bands of upwash
stretch a cove into an afternoon,
and deepen it to evening there, where ten
sandpipers race along the liquefaction's froth.
It beats, at their needling, a quick retreat; wherefrom they turn

three feet uphill to find
the last tide's hemline, run its whole cove-length of lacework back — then tack
and race and tack and
race again — the long and short of it is life for them, who poke
through frillwork at
such breakneck speed, make tracks like some unholy Underwood — till each
new tide-line's trove of trash

has been sandpipered, dashed along. The water now

is deadest low. What that
means, really, we can't know
by points of moment, or a pin,
or by the punctuator's time:
we need the binding
stitcheries of
syntax.

✧

Linking mechanisms in the universe produce

this woman who propels a baby-stroller
down the blacktop path, and runs behind it,
singing "Whee." The toddler in that suddenly

careening care
does a quick
chair-turn (her
patch of wild half-smile is not
unterrified, I see, beneath a tuft
of hair aloft); she cranes to check
the meaning of this new maternal
misdemeanor. Whereupon Mom whistles
"Whee" again — their smiles conspire — and then

they're gone. They've plunged beyond
my viewpoint. Vast as vision is, it's anchored
only in a sense: a starscape cast
about my minor part, the brooder on
the bench. But inch by inch the rising dark

makes any bench-mark run together
with the thought of them:
what's bolted, after all?

And what is fast?

Past All Understanding

The langouste's long feelers may be the result of a single gush of thought.
　　　　　　　　　　　　　　　　　　　　　—Ezra Pound

*For it is the opinion of choice virtuosi that the brain is only a crowd of little animals,
but with teeth and claws extremely sharp . . .*　　　　　　—Jonathan Swift

A woman there was balancing her baby
back-to-back. They held each other's hands,
did tilts and bends and teeter-totters on
each other's inclinations, making
casual covalency into
a human idiogram,
spontaneous Pilobolus —
a spectacle at which
the estimable Kooch
(half Border and half Lab)

began to bark. He wouldn't stop. The child slid off
the woman's back — now they were two again (and so
he quieted a bit). But they were two who
scowled and stared (now it was I who grew
disquieted). You looked,
I started to explain, like one

big oddity to him. (They weren't appeased.) He barks at
crippled people too. (Now they were horrified.) Meanwhile a wind

rose at the kiosk, stapled with yard jobs, sub-clubs, bands somebody named
for animals. The whole park fluttered up and flailed, and Kooch, unquenchable,
perceived the higher truth. The upshot: such a bout of barking
as to make the bicyclists bypassing (bent beneath their packs),
an assortment of teaching assistants (harried, earnest, hardly earning) —
and even the white-haired full professorships
all come to a halt, in the wake
of the wave of their tracks.

What brouhahas! What flaps!
To Kooch's mind, if you
could call it that,
the worst was
yet to come —

for looming overhead, a host of red and yellow kites appeared
intent on swooping even to the cowlicks of the humans — Were
these people blind? — that woman in pink, that man in blue, who
paused there in his purview, stupidly, to shake their heads? He thinks

we're in danger, I tried again
to reason with my fellow-man. But now the dog

was past all understanding; he was uncontainable. He burst
into a pure fur paroxysm, blaming the sky for all that we
were worth: he held his ground with four feet braced

against the overturning earth . . .

Moon and TV

The chimpanzee and her newborn
(a likeness in the drooped diminutive,
a shape at first she tries to raise from death
with breath from her two lips, and now
lets drop into the dirt, for want
of any glimmer of response) —
the two of them are on

TV. Or *in* it, I should say,
since *over* it there is a moon.
(The eye can't fathom these
transparencies in counterpoise,
like glasses in the sand, or wind
in windows, speech in spits,
constitutive.) One moon (to get

back to the unmade man) is
altogether over — and another dashed upon —
Lake Union (slick though the lake-face seems
with twilit swipes of sentiment and sail).
Should any lunar body rise

behind those forest chimpanzees
there'd be some four or maybe five
related forms, in just this one
reminded room. And which
is true? (You're on, says you.)
The moon right now

is measurably smaller than
the dead ape-baby's head.
But neither one can be revived,
however long it lolls
in earth's embrace. I know

my place. Unthinkably far-off, I am
the moon-monkey's semblable, caught in the same
sublunes of cycle — brought-up, let-down,
mob-summed, mum-sobbed, inmate of
a bleeding narrative, forever being
seized, released, shaken, mistaken,
molded to the mercies of
a mimic muscle —

spell-bent,
      heart-rent,
            spawn of a spondee . . .

One Woe

One woe is future, cast
from memory. And all our hours

went into it. All our engines
can't forestall it. One woe's past. (No woe

is pleasant: who would revel
in such revelations? How was any

woe begun?) No need
to wonder. One woe's present, so

it can't be done.

Three To's and an Oi

Cassandra's kind
of crying was

otototoi . . . They translate it
o woe is me, but really it's

less graspable than that — it isn't Greek for
nothing, all that stuttering in tones . . . When things get bad,

we baby-talk. In throes of terror in the night,
when dreads cannot be turned aside

by presences with promises, or dronings of a long
erroneous lullaby, or shorter story lines —

of which the lines themselves
have given rise to fear — we wake up

in Cassandra's kind
of quandary. There's been

some terrible mistake.
We're all about to die.

✦

Each whiplash of a girl, each eddy of a boy
comes reeling back from too much sheer

towardness — clarity from cataract — only to be
drawn in, again:

into tomorrow by today,
into the tune by gondolier,

into the two by two who turn
the bow toward torrents of *veyz mir*.

Fast

If he's the rock, then I'm the water.
If he's the water, I'm the wind.
If he's the wind, I must be moonlight
driven in wavelengths to rock.

Questions for the Moon

after Rainer Maria Rilke

O slender no-body, who gets you
pregnant every month?
Who makes you endlessly
(almost terrestrially)
preoccupied with your weight?

You draw the blood
of our pubescent girls.
But what are you mother of,
twelve times a year?

Will we be raising your light-children
inside us? (Inside myself,
I've made a find:

a tender crib, with golden trim,
that seems to me

your kind.)

The Father of the Predicaments

He came at night to each of us asleep
And trained us in the virtues we most lacked.
Me he admonished to return his stare
Correctly, without fear. Unless I could,
Unblinking, more and more incline
Toward a deep unblinkingness of his,
He would not let me rest. Outside
In the dark of the world, at the foot
Of the library steps, there lurked
A Mercury of rust, its cab half-lit.
(Two worldly forms who huddled there

Knew what they meant. I had no business
With the things they knew. Nor did I feel myself
Drawn back through Circulation into Reference,
Until I saw how blue I had become, by virtue
Of its five TVs, their monitors abuzz with *is*'s

Etymologies . . .)

For Raya

We were presumed
from humus, then exhumed;
we were the human kind,
dirt always clung to us.

✧

There is no opposite for sky.
There is no opposite for blue.
Nor for example is "We died"
exactly the negation of "we lived" —

once said, they turn alike
to lies: they can't
be said to be true.

✧

Once we were born, and now
we are born. God help me, for I feel

a lingering confusion at this
radical rewrite, the root retort, the claim
of presence to be lasting. All it turns upon

is us — the billions of us persons,
each an utmost, with a verb
to be — for whom

the being born is passive

only grammatically.

✧

No word can clear itself:
make itself clear.
The very saying's weak.

But I have lived, and I have died: such language
must be torn by its roots from someone else's
ventricles of throat: *she* could not speak.

Spill of Howl

The stripe of shine stays put, and yet
across its one lit track are driven
shimmerworks of wave —

the countless passing
through the one. It is the way
we see, the lay we're lent.
(The endlessness we can't

abide — we haven't
died —we have to be.)

✧

Poured forth from moon in one
broad corridor, this swath of mercury
(ubiquitously stirring) works the dark. What
wavelengths fasten there
(the there of that

befallen happenstance, given a moon full-blown, a current
near to flood, a wind-struck view
of shivers sur-subliminal, near pure
precision) no known

humankind would dare:
it's too bright black, and too fire-cold,
too senseless-silver
an authority.

✧

This ray is all
the eye's own stirring,
it's the eye's own dark that takes
(for the round world)
sides: one vocable,
one revocable.

✧

Meanwhile behind our backs
the eyehole of the stove is stoked
with burning tree, and anybody (even we)
can see it there, ahead of us. How can this be?

By blessed intervention! I mean you, my means,

unfathomably surfaced, and apparently unground:
who can (reflective) harbor
our whole burning, yet
(forgetful) let

the coldest otherness stream through:
o flow, my true
love, window,
by your virtue
all the turning airs, returning, do

begin a bay, beget a sound . . .

Ghazal of the Better-Unbegun

A book is a suicide postponed. —Cioran

Too volatile, am I? too voluble? too much a word-person?
I blame the soup: I'm a primordially
stirred person.

Two pronouns and a vehicle was Icarus with wings.
The apparatus of his selves made an ab-
surd person.

The sound I make is sympathy's: sad dogs are tied afar.
But howling I become an ever more un-
heard person.

I need a hundred more of you to make a likelihood.
The mirror's not convincing — that at-best in-
ferred person.

As time's revealing gets revolting, I start looking out.
Look in and what you see is one unholy
blurred person.

McHugh, you'll be the death of me — each self and second studied!
Addressing you like this, I'm halfway to the
third person.

So Thick?

Freud, presented with a copy of Wilhelm Reich's new book
The Function of the Orgasm, is said to have remarked "So thick?"

As thieves, as clotted cream, molasses poured in March,
or dullards duly quizzed, as thin's mate in
the marriage vow, or black fly hoverings
upon Katahdin, ketchup in the kitchen's
bottleneck, or traffic's slow red ooze
on I-5 every dusk, as musk
in the mind of an elephant,
or malice in the minds of men,
this treatise on the uses
of the human love-cramp

isn't surely anywhere as thick.
But what's the use of use, at this

imponderable juncture? Just
how practical are practices? Is poetry
poetic? And to what high end
the spondee's spasm? If the seizure leaves us
sobered up, we're lucky. Lucky

(after the humpback's beached) to have a bath
of modest aftermath, a tristesse to
redress the tryst! We're lucky to escape
the clutch of Sophocles' "furious master" (feeling's fist),
for the rest of the evening. A breather from breathing!
If the world for a merciful while be spared our craving,
or if spilling brine by brimfuls can
(for only the blink of an animal eye)
undo a few of our meaning's demeanings,
our siring's desirings, and give us one
pure moment's peace, I'd say the fucking
function's clear. One fewer war for now!

(Meanwhile, in the wombs
engorged with worm,
the drumroll starts
its endlessness again.
They'll come from some
deep months away,

the humped-up little beating forms of men . . .)

My Hexahedron Mated with His Cone

My hexahedron mated with his cone,
and made a form incapable of bearing
city life for six months at a stretch,
yet ever in the wilderness appearing

restless, of civilities bereft.
Half-lyric, half-tendentious, it could roll
around a cornered point, in Central Square;
or make a thumper's lumbering assault

on indecision, ending anywhere.
He needed other people to think ill
of people with. I needed only him.
To keep humanity's good name untried

(and therefore unconvicted) I would trim
my sex to rondelay. That's how we bred
our objectless geometry — applied
intransitives. One lay around, one lied.

The Starrier the Scarier

N.B.: A Love Poem

So it looks.
It seems to look.
Appears to seem.

All the more
in the mirror, for
example, on that mere

Mercedes, where a world could wing
a skyscape right away. Superlatives
of sheen on done! What do we take

arriving for? Only the best
asbestos, most expensive
avocado? (Juried show: hide

hung!) Among (Beckett is nothing
if he's not precise) — among! —
his adversary's testicles did Mercier

launch forth his boot . . .
And as for you, my sun
and moon, what

numb and numbest might apply?
How is it there inside, if there's
an inside to be had? (No

answers emanate from you.)
Say something moving, so I know
how far afoot (how far ahead!)

intendeds tend to go . . .

Wise Ease

You are not missing,
rather you are minded
in high tossings
and the best subtended

brain-branch, winded
bellow. Who could tell you
from my hollow sounding
well? The fall is lifelong, to

the knees. In real
told time (in subdivided sum)
I am your keeper — but in one whole
kingdom come I am

the kept. You swipe my dream —
who seem a seventh
of a quarter-moon, some
umpteenth heavening

afoot. Missing you're not—
although you went and took
my breath — but oh by every hook
an eye is missed. The very thought

(a double-you X'd out)
to death is kissed . . .

Out of Mind

Gentled through winters with too much rain,
coddled by moderate verdures (not a stick looks
dead in the dooryard — evergreens in broadleaf, set to trigger
big red outbursts — an embarrassment of riches!) — this is
paradise in February, so it's churlish, surely, to admit

I miss my heart's
austerer home. I miss
the knuckling down
on landscapes known
as necks and heads;
what's sharpened into
etcheries of age — arthritic
bush, twig dignity;
and so much un-
relenting sun
it puts its wings
on everything ten-plus
below (a tree in icy sheath
delivers shivers of exquisite
negativity). How choose

one's kind? Part-time I'm missing
all of somewhere else. My Maine is bone;
my west is flesh. The latter has no place
without the former, but the former
has a future out of mind.

Mens in the West

"Mind! Mind!
Mocking in mind!"
the madman said
who strode one then another
way about the parking lot.
He carried some infernal kind
of metal cone (was this
a weapon or a shield?
was it a metaphor?) which came
to its point in a bright red bulb.
From there a wire
ran to one ear (his right).
What couldn't such
an apparatus hear?
He was so bright, the passersby
averted all their gazes.

I hadn't for weeks been able to tell, in these parts,
two things apart — the homes from heliports,
the churches from the luncheonettes —
so subtle was the architecture of
a California distinction (humans having come
west, after all, to be blessed
with the absence of opposites).
Here, however, was this one near-human

spending not a moment's time on understatement.
Glaring, indiscreet, he was a form of nature,
sure as any hill-face
blackened to the whiskers,
sure as any wildfire hot for fame, sure as any
far-off star's reminding. Even, in the evening, sure as pure

Pacific: set upon, it's blinding.

If Only

How much can a brain stem
stem? It cannot stop the sucker up —
(What a nasty penchant for make-work!)
Lazing, teasing, it's been known to let

the ghost braids of a brainy efflorescence
drain down-spine: I talk a sudden red streak,
or see blue. Deep in the night I'm made
to doze, so it can play the traffic-cop

to rumblings forth and streamings back
from headquarters to factory, from cablelink to coil:
oil-rig details, appointments with the plumber I still
(slumbering) must keep. But just

as soon as I'm awake, I mind
myself. I do my breathing
differently, or so console myself,
decide on deep or shallow as I wish,

contain myself, have worlds to supervise,
as my own calling calls for. IT cannot imagine
what I go through! Every phototropic day,
the work of waving, leaving, flowering,

cross-pollination! All IT knows
is how to bode and rummage.
It's a duodenal high-brow,
overhung, root-bound,

with no hope but the blind. If only it
would stem, would really stem!
Take a load off my being! my mind
off my mind!

Streaming Audio

A writer is somebody for whom writing is more difficult than it is for other people.
—Thomas Mann

The thought can hurt. It runs the mindbed,
underwrites the waves. It means to come
as close to real as possible. No real
is possible. It means to come
too close. Its hosts are on

alert. Its paths aren't idio — but neither can
you keep its time. It lingers in
a special sense, the kind that kind
of kills. It seems to some
as possible as ever

real was close to close. No real
is closable. It dreams of drumming Innisfree,
but seems to mean it's live.
To last it has

to flow, and so
to stream it has to strive.

Sun Grounded in Sky-Pool

It isn't in itself a thing is known—
en soi pour soi applies its sauce to sauce
and all the increments of living bone
amount to marrow-making: rounder loss.
Where would a self be best advised to look
for self-assurance? Where put emptiness?
How move the mind to awe, its best address?
Can wonder come to life (whose breath we took)?

In the Japanese garden the bee's regard
begins to fumble, fondle, multiply.
Unthinkabilities *are* seen: but hardly
have the surfaces seduced the eye
than every curve begets its wave of thought.
The mind is blinded, so the heart goes out.

Dust Jacket

October 1987: Robert O'Donnell raises baby Jessica from a well-shaft
April 1995: Robert O'Donnell kills himself

Not quite a name — sort of a named —
or something namish — he's
gone out at last without
his coat. What once

they viewed and inter-
viewed, a pull
from the well of a pipe,
(his throat), became

the depression in which he could rest
a rifle. Better to keep
things quiet, live deep down
in richly un-

synopsized dark. Above, we come
to the sickness of wishes,
lust in a flash, a fletch,
a damage flesh

would rather bequeath than be
made heir to. Game goes gamey,
lackey lackish. After the soft life — fast at first —
turned only fastish — he the hero only of the moment

took his pick-up truck, and left
his jacket back at home.
(It takes some kind
of wife to make

reports like these). The rest
is history, which happens,
if it has to,
in the woods

where one is mortified enough
to put the last big thought-hole
in one's head-hole, timed
to turn all names to verb-blast —

famed to famish.

Verdict

You don't know what I was thinking,
he began. I said I didn't think I did,
although I knew he sometimes
thought we thought alike.
That he believed we wouldn't now
I had to wonder why he said. It isn't your

believing I was thinking of, he answered; it is knowing
I was wondering about. Now I was sure
he meant what I believed, but then
I wondered whether both
or one were true. I knew
I meant to think it
through. But mean
means quite one thing alone,

and quite another with another; surely I was right to think
he knew how well we meant. Apparently
he didn't, or I wasn't. One of us
is wrong, that's evident, but who?
By all that's just, adjudicate: the only un-

committed one is you.

Neitherer Brings Charges

The white pigs work but cannot play. With black pigs, vice is verse.
Between us boys (between their inks and ois)

how can these animals communicate? The dogs eat dog, they love
their *chien sauté.* (In Aristophanes, they say *Au! au!* The lambkin

begs *Bé-bé.*) In all your languages, the mule will balk,
the men will beat the living

devil from the beast. Take snakes: they're everywhere
because they've no impediment of legs; they do not have

to stand to sneak. And think of time's
two-timing ways — it fathers years,

and falls in weeks. When someone barks out
Author! author! — thinking thinking's

in the wings, however far the furor goes
no star will come: only a fever

in the audience — the fighters and the fuckers,
those who take, and those who give. There's room

for one kind or the other, half of all
Binarydom should live. It's man

or mudlover— you take your pick. It's
logos or it's low. We cannot be

at one unless you choose.
(In Heraclitus, what are twos,

but war?) It's them or us, it's
yes or no, it's time-the-father

or it's pussy-whipped. I tell you outright,
I'm a neitherer. But what are you? You are a bother.

Sizing

Where's my hairbrush? Where's the belt?
I want my switch. I need that cane. Just let me get
my hands upon that licking-stick, and then

we'll take the starch right out of you.
Your hide is fixing for a tanning. Just you wait.
What hit you you won't know. The future cannot help

but cut you down to size. Its feeling for you,
more and more apparently parental,
cannot help but grow.

The Brink

Spruced right up to the brink, the cliff
falls off. In radicalized hunks it
drops itself (such is an oracle's artillery)
onto its own downfallen kind:
bull's-eyes of rock-shock below!

Down there, on a seaside shelf,
the human being who had taken
time out, dreaming slow, from nine
lives never finished, up in the Castle of If,

sees in a flash (neither meaning nor mind)
the destiny of drives. The drift.

The Gulf Between the Given and the Gift

Between the driven and the drift, you're moved —
whether air, or a cattle-prod, does it.
Art, said the naturalist, in heaven.
Said the blind: Long time no touch. The hooker interjected:
Come again. But I, I was once more unable

even to converse. (I could not get the lion
out of mind, intending to tear a gazelle
from the love of the leap of her life.) There was much
we would catch. There was much we would miss.
There was some we would have to do twice.

Not So Fast

I thought my life was
my intelligence. But then a dimming overcame me,

then a wind, and then the whole
sound waveletted, aroused.
I was extremely gradual in my
misgiving, as I looked (for things did not
look) up — and there the buffeted

high race of K's revealed, so that a man could
see it for himself, the fabled column in the clouds
(which theretofore I'd only known
from books): and it had one
long eyehole through it
to a blue too light

to trust. (The lightest blue is heaven's kind
of founding oxymoron.) It's not there
for us to understand; it's there for us
to be looked down on through . . .

How clumsily I made my way
upstairs from shore to cover —
where a forest took my thrashing for me.
Still, I'd had my awful

eyeful of the future, in which we
are bearing up for life, while it
bears down, a mind for legalism,
slow. It has the time. (Forget
your airs.) It has the grounds.

A Night Is All

We struck it rough:
the racked wave gave off
cloud-lengths; at the cliff
a tree-trio broke in half

its fourth: a peckered stump.
We struck it up, we camped
our hewn gold here and there in clumps
of pine, we loved our honest lamps

all night. But who out of our dreaming woke
and moaned? Who took
a look at us, and saw the slack
sex, tuckered cheek?

Who stole a cold reminder, stayed
his ardor, stood his ground (that undegraded
heaven?) It was you, in my half-made

mind-bed; and it was I, in your unwavering
unfoundedness. That hurt a lover
could not leap. That luck a diver

could not sound.
To get forever its renown,
it takes a soul or two around

a night.

Ein Ander

Beyond the tree's red bullet-sprays
the bay is braving
slate and slater shades
until the sun

is tanked entirely,
spilling *huile de* bruise
across an eyeful's cove.
And still we stay. The blues
black out. And still we are not blind.
Some starfires sharpen up. It isn't

risk, it's imminence we run.
What's done by heart to day can still

be done to night by mind.

The Water

took time to calm, but when
its surfaces had settled on a face,
the image went far down into
its one lit lens —

her head shone deepest in and farthest off,
its long hair dripping needlepoints
up toward her eyes. (The world was out-
side down or topside in: Rosettas broken
leave one un-

intelligible.) At the surface drank
(companionable, tip to tip, accustomed to
a partnership) two breasts, each
with its other, a practical
endlessness, poured

from a pair. This was mesmer
to terrify mortals: and so
from the calm of corroborate tubworlds
she climbed out, bore her own
dead weight again, took on the old

mundane emergency: the world
at large, its separations
hefted. As she rose, her lightness
fell away; it wound from her
in coilworks and in threadworks spun of time,

it swept in shining down and fell
behind (in some event-
uality). Now it was clear
who was blind.

Deposition of the Seer

I burned the arrows
then I burned the air.

I burned the boats
the bay was taking

for a mere mirage. I took them for
a fact. I saw a sway rise up

from gold to red, and red to black —
I saw the sway, I couldn't hold it.

Whose ring was that, whose the wiry hand? And
by the bye who added good? To hell who added

O? The curves went wavery, and lit the whole
world's neighborhood. And then the sun went

out. That was a message from
the bull's-eye to the bow.

A Salt: Three Variations on Five Senses

a worn knobbed stick between his legs to keep off dogs —William Carlos Williams

1.
a sip, a whiff,
a glimpse of the single
unsung note (a dangle
between doubles, bare
as earshot's sheer
ephemerality),
a wing across
a fingertip

2.
a gulp from the gutter, a snort from the shovel:
eyeloads gobbled and the shelves of self
all helped to heaps
of heaving overtones:
a muddy mind, immodest, and
five himalayas of massage

3.
in light of all of this,
best just, to taste, take in (inhale)
detecting's cast: the wave-point brings
to mind an eye: to ear a shell: to hand
a ring. you are yourself
a sailed-in fact, a tact in things.

Cartographer at Home

1. Gin Cove Road, 1997

Golds beyond degree have sunk
to new September lows, sent stripes across
a hundred trunks, for one

hour only, codes to deepest moss.
In open fields, deciduousness does
brisk businesses in crosshatch. Were you to be drawn

past forest to the shore, your fur about your ears, you'd read
long volumes in the cliff's descent: through nine horizons
(age of pebble, age of shale)

a lean subversive root has struck
its lyric, corkscrewed vertical. The beach
is one big wedge. It makes

its hard point underwater, but it keeps
its uplands fluted (evidence of decades
failing at a dune). Upon this higher composition,

skeins of black egg-sac and olive tatter
twist their best successions of remark. The beach
has lured into its sandhold something

hacked-off, root-like, ten feet wide,
and tipped it over, and begun to swallow it:
half of the muscular tangle protrudes

above the fluent strand. Such countlessness
is script: unfathomable, yet exact. Impressed
into a mere episteme, the few

become a future, and the littoral
a literature. In suffix, much is made
of what — at root — was born (like Nat and Mort,

the landlords of the mind). I haven't so much
grounds for thought, as thought for grounds:
the knuckles, needles, ledges of

a calligraphic bent. O
better me, my letters! (Let
the link be rent.)

2. Ghoti

The gh comes from rough, the o from women's,
and the ti from unmentionables — presto, it's a Shavian
cuisine: a mystery: a fish. Our wish was for
a better revelation, for a correspondence — if not lexical, at least

phonetic; if not with Madonna
then at least with Mary Magdalene.
Instead we get the sheer
opacity of things: an accident of incident,

a tracery of history: the dung inside the dungarees,
the jock strap for a codpiece, and the ruined patches
bordering the lip. One high-heeled boot could make
Sorrento sorry, Capri corny, even little Italy

a little ill. In lower case, a lover looks
one over — egg uneasy, semen without oars —
and there, on board, tricked out in fur and fin,
the landlubber who wound up captain. Where's it going,

this our HMS? More west? More forth? The quest
itself is at a long and short behest: it's wound in winds.
(Take rough from seas, and women from the shore,
unmentionables out of mind. A minute of millennium

is still a long unculminating stint,
a stonish monument: my god,
what's utterable? Gargah, gatto, goat?) As animals,
for animals, we seine and trawl and drag and gaff our way

around the everloving globe — dig mains,
lay lines, book passages. But earth remains
untranslated, unplumbed. A million herring run where we
catch here a freckle, there a pock. The depths to which things live

words only glint at. Terns in flight work up
what fond minds might call syntax; as for that
semantic antic in the distance, is it whiskered fish,
finned cat? Forget the words, the world is too

amazing to be true, if oceans can be flown
and skies swum through.

3. Upshot

Forget the low world of the windowsill, the one I didn't wash.
Forget its web of dessicated fly, its etchery of dust; and see yourself

outside instead: for there the bush (the galed, regaled, and thrashing
bush,
the rose she planted when she wasn't dead) with all its billions

of serrations makes
a decade tremble. Call it

one thing, if you must— rugosa, in a simple stand.
But monoliths have molecules.

And if you lift your eyes again, about a latitude above,
your eyelines stream into the satins, lateral, that make

a bay a verb. Its volumes speak
of underlying depth — adverting to a whirlpool, it

is arabic for time. Outcropped from all
that running commentary there's

a line of molar scrubble — islands we identify
by things no longer there — like Cherry, Indian, and Deer —

and rising out of that (in more than mere
appearance) is the venerable

sky. O holy sky! O eminence of haze! Your
mountains gallop and your pourings puff —

your spackle has a delicacy, and your hatch a ladderworks —
o sky, our haven of high nines, accumulated candyville, our

whiff of glimmer — you preferrer of a bloody osprey
to our huddlers on a limb — preparer of

our best and last rebuff: unbreathability.
O everybody's air, nobody's home! Since flesh

cannot be saved, supply for love
a fairer figure, finer ground. Make zero

absolute. Set nothing thereabove.

Nano-Knowledge

There, a little right
of Ursus Major, is
the Milky Way:
a man can point it out,
the biggest billionfold of all
predicaments he's in:
his planet's street address.

What gives? What looks
a stripe a hundred million
miles away from here

is where we live.

✧

Let's keep it clear. The Northern Lights
are not the North Star. Being but
a blur, they cannot reassure us.
They keep moving — I think far
too easily. September spills

some glimmers of
the boreals to come:
they're modest pools
of horizontal haze, where later

they'll appear as foldings in the vertical,
a work of curtains, throbbing dim
or bright. (One wonders at
one's eyes.) The very sight
will angle off in glances or in shoots
of something brilliant, something

bigger than we know, its hints uncatchable
in shifts of mind . . . So there

it is again, the mind, with its
old bluster, its self-centered
question: what

is dimming, what is bright?
The spirit sinks and swells, which cannot tell
itself from any little luster.

Open Air

Once it streamed
through dream-

shrines (unseen,
not untrue): voluptuous, the spleen

reddened at the thought — i.e. the shadow — of
ulteriority. The liver livened, love-

struck. Scarlets glittered in his guttering
arterials, and through his foggy matter

passed a quick pink flush. Of his life, the air
(apprised) was then, for life, by lungfuls evermore reprised; and of his
glare

the twice-burned sun was pilfered. Parts
were memorized (brain stemmed, lymph known). He could by heart

mean something in a branching universe. What might
he mean today? His transitives are blown, his naves are blue. About

his overalled physique (which once was strapping
and today is only strapped) the greens grow more

and more unmowed. About his dead body outdoors,
enormous sky arranges little flappings.

Interior

after Paul Valéry

With sidewise eyes and swaying chains
a slave restores the vase-pools, swims
through nearby mirrors, makes a pass
at mysteries of bed with her

unsullied hands. She puts a woman
in the middle of my room,
a decent one, who comes and goes
about my long reflection's lattice,

passes through my stare without
its absence being shattered —
as a filter over sun will spare

pure reason its own apparatus.

Qua Qua Qua

Philosophical duck, it takes
some fine conjunctive paste to put
this nothing back together, gluing glue to glue —

a fine conjunction, and a weakness too
inside the nature of the noun. O duck, it doesn't
bother you. You live in a dive, you daub the lawn,

you dabble bodily aloft: more wakes
awake, where sheerness shares
its force. The hot air moves

you up, and then
the cool removes. There's no
such thing as things, and as for *as*:

it's just an alias, a form of time,
a self of other, something between thinking
and a thought (one minds his mom,

one brains his brother). You seem
so calm, o Cain of the corpus callosum,
o fondler of pondlife's fallopian gore,

knowing nowheres the way we don't
dare to, your web-message
subjectless (nothing a person could

pray or pry predicates from). From a log
to a logos and back, you go flinging
the thing that you are — and you sing

as you dare — on a current of
nerve. On a wing
and a wing.

Etymological Dirge

'Twas grace that taught my heart to fear.

Calm comes from burning.
Tall comes from fast.
Comely doesn't come from come.
Person comes from mask.

The kin of charity is whore,
the root of charity is dear.
Incentive has its source in song
and winning in the sufferer.

Afford yourself what you can carry out.
A coward and a coda share a word.
We get our ugliness from fear.
We get our danger from the lord.

Acknowledgments

Grateful acknowledgement is made to the following journals and magazines, which published poems now collected in *The Father of the Predicaments*:

"Not Unterrified" (under the title "Carriage Return") and "Were They Hurt" were originally published in *Faultline*, then reprinted in *Southern Indiana Review*.

"Past All Understanding" (under the title "Flap Copy") and "Three Variations on Five Senses" (under the title "In Several Senses") were published in *The Denver Quarterly*.

"Moon and TV" and "Dust Jacket" were published by *Seneca Review*.

"One Woe" appeared in *River City Journal*.

"Three To's and an Oi," "Neitherer Brings Charges," and "The Starrier the Scarier" were published in *Verse*.

"Fast" appeared in *The Progressive*.

"The Father of the Predicaments," "Streaming Audio," "Qua *Qua* Qua," and "Sizing" appeared in *Meridian*; "Qua *Qua* Qua" then subsequently appeared in *Jefferson Monthly*.

"A Salt: Three Variations on Five Senses" was published in *Connecticut Review*.

"The Father of the Predicaments," "A Salt: Three Variations on Five Senses," and "Etymological Dirge" were republished in *Contemporary American Poetry: A Bread Loaf Anthology*, ed. Michael Collier.

"Spill of Howl" (under the title "Way Out") was published in *Green Mountain Review*.

"So Thick?" (under the title "Freud, Presented with a Copy of Wilhelm Reich's New Book") and "Sun Grounded in Sky-Pool" were published in *Paris Review*.

"My Hexahedron Mated with His Cone" appeared in *Fence*.

"Mens in the West " was published in *Teacup*.

"If Only" appeared in *Seattle Review*.

"The Brink" (under the title "Past Part") appeared in *Indiana Review*.

Parts of "The Gulf Between the Given and the Gift" appeared in *Urbanus/Raizzir*.

"Not So Fast" was published in *Gargoyle Magazine*.

"*Ein ander*" ("Beyond the tree's red bullet-sprays") appeared in *Pequod*.

"The Water" was published in *Oregon Review*; originally it appeared in *Columbia (A Magazine)*, under the title "Unbroken Water."

"Deposition of the Seer" appeared in *Partisan Review*, under the title "Deposition."

Part 1 of the larger poem entitled "Cartographer at Home" appeared under the title "Gin Cove" in *Marlboro Review*; Part 2 of "Cartographer at Home" was published in

Third Coast under the title "Ghoti."

"The Interior" (after Valéry) was originally published in *Colorado Review*.

"Open Air" appeared in ZYZZYVA.

"Etymological Dirge" appeared in *The American Scholar*.

I owe a debt of gratitude to the Lila Wallace/Reader's Digest Award Foundation, and to the University of Washington in Seattle, which affords me the kind of time most productive of writing and most protective of contemplation.

UNIVERSITY PRESS OF NEW ENGLAND publishes books under its own imprint and is the publisher for Brandeis University, Dartmouth College, Middlebury College, University of New Hampshire, Tufts University, and Wesleyan University Press.

ABOUT THE AUTHOR   Heather McHugh is Milliman Distinguished Writer-in-Residence and Professor of English at the University of Washington in Seattle. She also regularly teaches in the low-residency MFA Program at Warren Wilson college, near Asheville, N.C., and at the Writers' Workshop of the University of Iowa. She is the author of five books of poetry: *Hinge & Sign: Poems, 1968–1993* (Wesleyan, 1994), *Shades* (Wesleyan, 1988), *To the Quick* (Wesleyan, 1987), *A World of Difference* (Houghton Mifflin, 1981), and *Dangers* (Houghton Mifflin, 1977). She has translated two volumes of poetry: *Because the Sea Is Black: Poems by Blaga Dimitrova* (with co-translator Nikolai Popov, Wesleyan, 1989) and *D'Après Tout: Poems by Jean Follain* (Princeton, 1982). Her version of Euripides' *Cyclops* (with an introduction by David Konstan) is forthcoming in a new series from Oxford University Press. in 1999 she was elected a chancellor of the Academy of American Poets.

Library of Congress Cataloging-in-Publication Data
McHugh, Heather, 1948–
The father of the predicaments / Heather McHugh.
p.   cm. — (Wesleyan Poetry)
ISBN 0–8195–6386–2 (alk. paper)
PS3563.A311614F38 1999
811'.54—dc21   99-14234